U.S. NAVY

BY NICK GORDON

BELLWETHER MEDIA · MINNEAPOLIS MN

EPIC BOOKS are no ordinary books. They burst with intense action, high-speed heroics, and shadows of the unknown. Are you ready for an Epic adventure?

This edition first published in 2013 by Bellwether Media, Inc.

No part of this publication may be reproduced in whole or in part without written permission of the publisher. For information regarding permission, write to Bellwether Media, Inc., Attention: Permissions Department, 5357 Penn Avenue South, Minneapolis, MN 55419.

Library of Congress Cataloging-in-Publication Data

Gordon, Nick.
 U.S. Navy / by Nick Gordon.
   p. cm. (Epic books: U.S. military)
 Includes bibliographical references and index.
 Summary: "Engaging images accompany information about the U.S. Navy. The combination of high-interest subject matter and light text is intended for students in grades 2 through 7"–Provided by publisher.
   Audience: Ages 6-12.
 ISBN 978-1-60014-830-9 (hbk. : alk. paper)
 1. United States. Navy–Juvenile literature. I. Title.
 VA58.4.G67 2013
 359.00973–dc23   2012008563

Printed in the United States of America, North Mankato, MN.

TABLE OF CONTENTS

THE U.S. NAVY

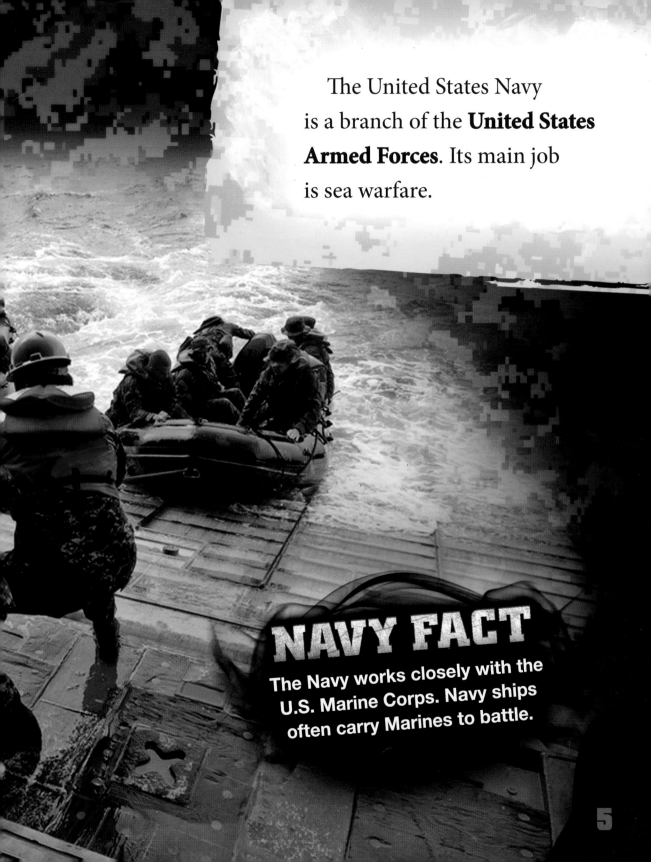

The United States Navy is a branch of the **United States Armed Forces**. Its main job is sea warfare.

NAVY FACT

The Navy works closely with the U.S. Marine Corps. Navy ships often carry Marines to battle.

UNITED STATES NAVY

Founded: 1775

Headquarters: Arlington, Virginia

Motto: "Honor, Courage, Commitment"

Size: More than 300,000 active personnel

Major Engagements: Revolutionary War, War of 1812,
                        American Civil War, World War I,
                        World War II, Korean War,
                        Vietnam War, Gulf War, Iraq War,
                        War on Terror

The Navy uses ships and aircraft to perform **missions**. It has the largest **fleet** of ships in the world.

NAVY VEHICLES

AIRCRAFT CARRIER

Ships are the backbone of the Navy. Six to ten ships form a **carrier group**. The main ship is an **aircraft carrier**.

SHIPS IN A CARRIER GROUP

Aircraft Carrier....

Destroyer ....

Cruiser ....

Submarine ....

Supply Ship ....

DESTROYER

CRUISER

Cruisers and destroyers are fighting ships. They carry guns, **missiles**, and **torpedoes**.

Submarines can go deep below the surface of the ocean. They spy on enemy ships and fire missiles and torpedoes.

SUBMARINE

MISSILE

13

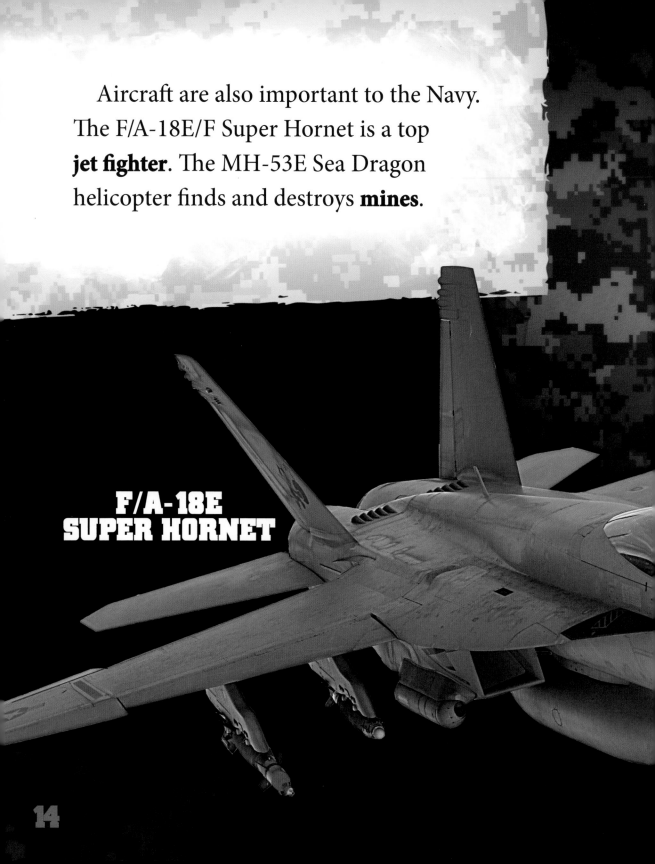

Aircraft are also important to the Navy. The F/A-18E/F Super Hornet is a top **jet fighter**. The MH-53E Sea Dragon helicopter finds and destroys **mines**.

F/A-18E
SUPER HORNET

MH-53E
SEA DRAGON

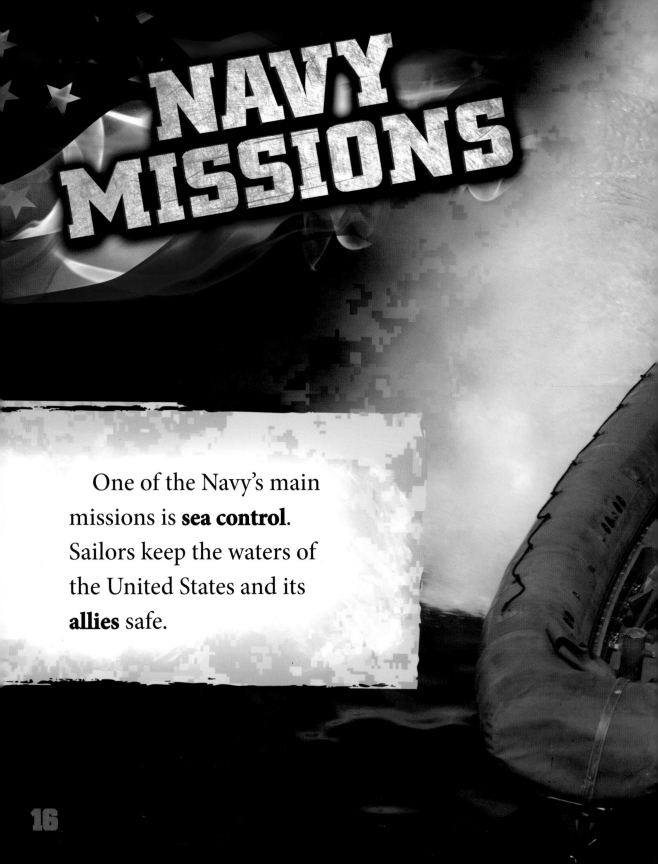

NAVY MISSIONS

One of the Navy's main missions is **sea control**. Sailors keep the waters of the United States and its **allies** safe.

The Navy also carries out attack missions. Ships and aircraft fire guns and missiles at enemies.

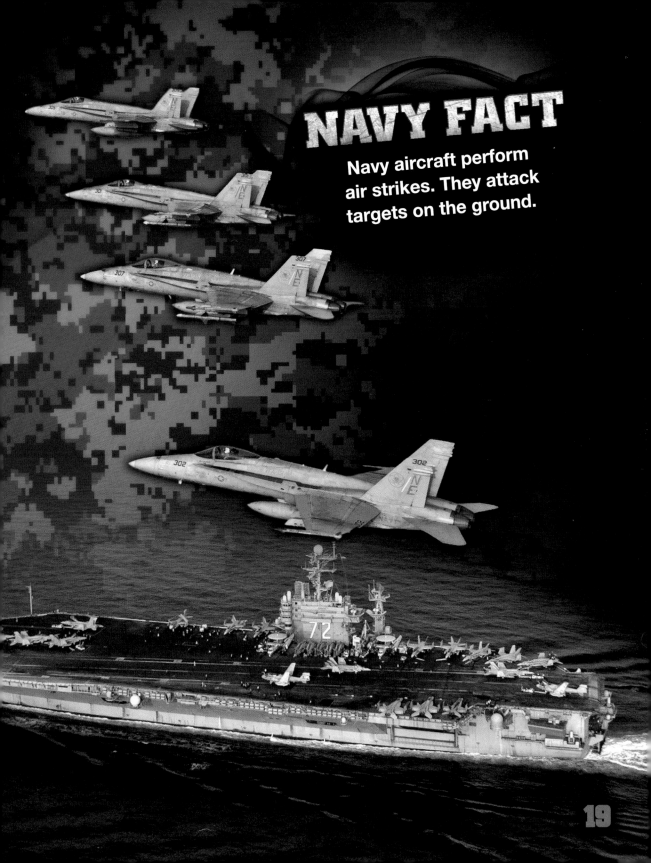

NAVY FACT

Navy aircraft perform air strikes. They attack targets on the ground.

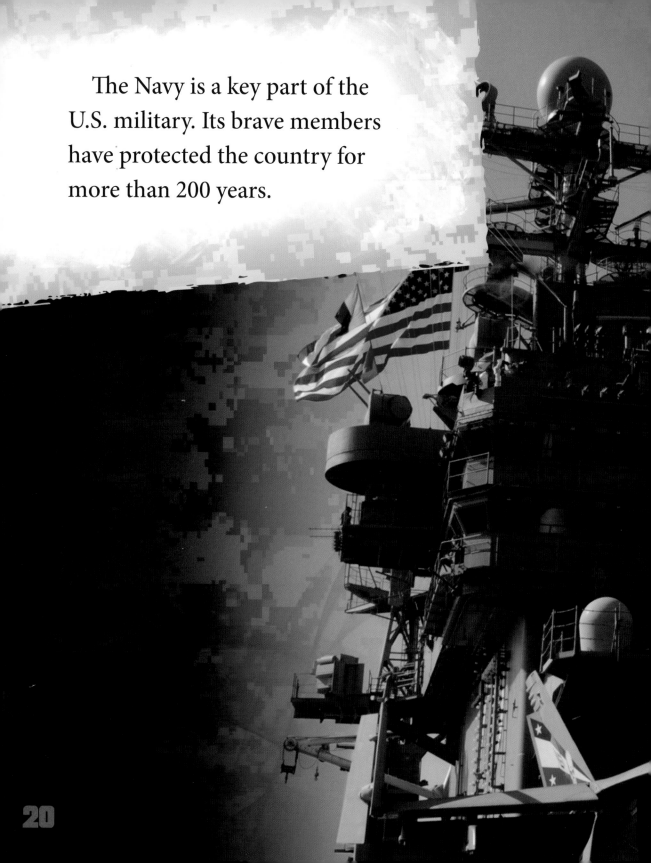

The Navy is a key part of the U.S. military. Its brave members have protected the country for more than 200 years.

21

GLOSSARY

aircraft carrier—the largest ship within a Navy carrier group; planes take off from and land on aircraft carriers.

allies—friendly nations that have common goals or purposes; the United States has many allies around the world.

carrier group—a group of ships that travel and fight together

fleet—a large collection of ships under the same control

jet fighter—a fighter plane that has jet engines

mines—hidden explosives that go off when a person or vehicle touches or gets near them

missiles—explosives that are guided to a target

missions—military tasks

sea control—having military control of the sea

torpedoes—explosives that travel underwater toward targets

United States Armed Forces—the five branches of the United States military; they are the Air Force, the

TO LEARN MORE

At the Library

David, Jack. *United States Navy*. Minneapolis, Minn.: Bellwether Media, 2008.

Gordon, Nick. *Navy SEALs*. Minneapolis, Minn.: Bellwether Media, 2013.

Zobel, Derek. *Nimitz Aircraft Carriers*. Minneapolis, Minn.: Bellwether Media, 2009.

On the Web

Learning more about the U.S. Navy is as easy as 1, 2, 3.

1. Go to www.factsurfer.com.

2. Enter "U.S. Navy" into the search box.

3. Click the "Surf" button and you will see a list of related Web sites.

With factsurfer.com, finding more information is just a click away.

INDEX